Toronto, We Love You...
Volume 1

Printed and bound in Canada by Heritage Press Company Limited.

ISBN 0-88924-006-X

"The Brunswick House"

Drawings by	R.F.M.McInnis
Poetry by	Deborah J. Godin
Editor	Rolf Kalman
Designer	Catherine P. Wilson

Published and distributed by Simon & Pierre Publishing Company Limited,
P.O. Box 280 Adelaide Street Postal Station, Toronto M5C 1J0, Ontario.

When I arrived in Canada about twenty years ago, with my little satchel and my great expectations, I landed in Toronto.

If one emigrates, one should have the pioneer spirit — and if one has the pioneer spirit, one should be willing to pioneer. This is challenging and exciting, at least on the face of it. Grey dullness, restrictions, and a feeling of being closed in — in a town which, strangely enough, is open in all four directions — is not something which fosters the pioneer spirit.

And Toronto twenty years ago was one of the most boring places I had run across on several continents. It was boring because Toronto twenty years ago managed to hide all the assets she had——Hart House, the Arts and Letters Club, the Art Gallery, the Museum——under a unique and unobtrusive greyness. Indeed, Toronto was the only town I had ever come across which could hide the most poetic and beautiful outlet a city can have — her waterfront and the endless panorama of the lake — behind indescribable industrial rubbish.

The only cheerful thing was the general description of Toronto as "Hog Town", because at least I felt that there were brothers similarly thinking!

Today, twenty years later, I can't imagine living anywhere else but here. This is not to say that I am not aware of the rest of the world, and it certainly is not to say that the city has achieved the optimum in every aspect. What it does say is that, all things being equal, as an absolute standard, Toronto today is the best place to live in.

For a town — and a mediocre town — to grow into a city — and an outstanding city — in twenty short years is close to a miracle. In those twenty years, a skyline appeared out of nothing; the islands and High Park became international showcases, not only for elegance in gardening, but for accommodating hundreds of thousands of people in an atmosphere very few cities can offer. An industry grew, if not out of nothing, at least out of very little, which can and does support millions of people, and people came to Toronto to create this Utopia.

If Canada is a mosaic of nationalities and cultures, then surely this city has succeeded in becoming the focal point of this mosaic. If industrial growth is a measure of success, then surely Toronto is one of the most successful cities in the world.

But to put a restraint, a voluntary one, on growth for growth's sake, is what gives Toronto her ultimate and unique value.

First the shells were built, and the shells were necessary because they accommodated people. But once the shells were built, the people took over again. Those who had built the shells wanted to live a life — a life both human and humane. So after a history of less than a hundred years, this metropolis now not only houses a gigantic industrial empire, and skyscrapers and thruways and subways and whatever else goes with them, but also the National Ballet of Canada; the National Ballet School; the

Canadian Opera Company; one of the world's outstanding museums, and in the near future one of the showcase art galleries of the world; the world-famous Science Centre; Ontario Place on the waterfront — another international showcase; and virtually scores of thriving theatres, at a time when many other cities have a problem just to maintain what they established decades and even centuries ago.

Bay Street is Canada's financial heart and with all its complexities and intricacies in a free society, it is a much criticized but obviously vital organ. To make good on Bay Street, wherever you come from in Canada, is the final golden seal of approval.

The Annex — one square mile in the heart of downtown Toronto — is the balance.

The restraint, the break against growth for its own sake, the sanity, the human element and the voice of those who demand that the time has come, now that the shells are built, that they want to live in the shells.

The Annex is the most progressive part of Toronto because at an age when furiously-built industry can create nothing else but an additional drain on an already desperate fuel shortage, it creates artisans: artisans who can take a piece of leather and make shoes and bags and coats out of it; artisans who take raw wax and make beautiful candles; artisans who spin and weave, and hand-print books — who demand stores where the owner knows you and knows what you want; ushers in the little theatres who say hello to you rather than pushing you hysterically into your numbered seat, — and, by God, cops who behave like policemen.

For fifty years the Annex Ratepayers Association has tried to keep this area — in spite of developers, city planners and others — as a refuge for humans, for people.

In Toronto's history, fifty years is a very long time — almost an indication of outdatedness — and yet the Annex is avant garde. By planning or coincidence, in the heart of the big city, "neighbourhood" can exist. It is possible, towards the end of the twentieth century, to create an atmosphere where the facelessness of numbers has to take second place to those who created the numbers.

If Toronto is rapidly becoming a catalyst in Canada for all kinds of aspirations, so the Annex is becoming the spiritual home of those who seek to keep this imperative balance.

A community like this doesn't need a 'club' — it develops, indeed evolves, the classical meeting place in the classical Greek manner.

The Brunswick House is this meeting place.

Deborah J. Godin and Robert McInnis are Annex people. They write and draw in a way which reflects the feeling and the things which matter.

Rolf Kalman
Editor

Ye Olde Brunswick House

Ye Olde Brunswick House

BRUNSWICK HOUSE

Editor   Rolf Kalman

Designer   Catherine P. Wilson

The Brunswick House by night.
Photo by Bill Hannant.

Poet **Deborah J. Godin** was born in Detroit, but her grandparents were Maritimers and all through her early years she was deeply conscious of the Canadian element in her family, and made frequent trips to Canada to visit relatives and friends.

Deborah has always been interested in writing, in expressing her feelings and impressions with words. She also draws and has a special interest in art history; she received her B.A. in sculpture and art history from Western Michigan University, and her M.A. in art history from Wayne State University Graduate School. She loved her studies and continued them far beyond the point necessary to obtain her degrees. Her feelings about art, about the history of art, about writing, and about her own work in particular, are clear and simple: "Self-discipline is a beautiful thing", she believes — and she lives and works according to this belief.

Many visits to the city developed Deborah's love for Toronto, and as a result, she emigrated to Canada and now lives and works in the Annex. She has written a great deal about the city and its people; recently some of her illustrated poems were part of a show at York University. She shares Robert McInnis' special feeling for the Brunswick Tavern, and has written about the tavern and its people in lucidly beautiful and understanding verse. She may consider herself highly disciplined, but her sensitivity and humour shine through her clear words, making her her own best example of philosophy to which she subscribes.

Robert McInnis started to draw in Grade I — filling the margins of his arithmetic book with copies of the sailboats his teacher had drawn on the blackboard to teach the class to count. He drew all through his school career; studied art under Fred Ross and D. Edwin Campbell at Saint John Vocational School in New Brunswick (where he was born), and received his diploma in Fine and Applied Arts in 1961.

Art has pervaded his whole life since; during a stint in the RCAF, he was represented in the Canadian Forces Art Contests of 1965 and 1966; his work has been shown at the Vancouver Art Gallery, at Prince George College, at the College of New Caledonia, the Edmonton Art Gallery — and in 1972, he had his first one-man show of thirty portraits at the Burnaby Art Gallery in British Columbia.

He believes implicitly in the discovery and development of artistic individuality and personal creative expression as the true basis of art, as opposed to learned techniques or borrowed formulae. It was to foster this feeling that he was instrumental — and indeed highly influential — in the formation of THE GROUP, a small gathering of other artists who shared his feelings.

Robert McInnis makes no secret of his profound admiration for the great Toulouse Lautrec; and coming to Toronto to seek his own version of the "Moulin Rouge", he stumbled upon the Brunswick House Tavern — and disliked it intensely.

But it was close to where he lived, and he had the insight and intelligence to re-visit it from time to time until the unique and special quality of the Brunswick began to take hold of him. He became a familiar figure to the regulars, easily recognized under his tartan tam, as he sat quietly drawing, and drinking his beer — and now his love affair with the Brunswick is to take shape in the form of a sketchbook of drawings accompanied by poems.

Robert McInnis has done some writing of his own. "The Renegade's Lament", a long illustrated poem published this year by Fiddlehead Poetry Books in Fredericton, N.B., edited by Fred Cogswell, is a recent triumph. But he spends his time doing what he loves best — drawing — and has proved to his satisfaction that "you can make a living as an artist in Toronto". And in spite of his friends' affectionate description of him as "Canada's most successful unknown artist", it is only a question of time when the 'unknown' will be rectified.

THE BRUNSWICK TAVERN IS NOT ANOTHER
NEON
AMPLIFIED
YONGE STRIP
SHOWBAR
THE KIND YOU
DON'T ASK
YOUR MAMA FIRST
CAN YOU GO
THERE

NOT
SOME DARK
ETHNIC
HIDEAWAY
STRANGE
MUSIC AND
ATMOSPHERE
A NEIGHBOURHOOD
PUB FROM
AN UNFAMILIAR
NEIGHBOURHOOD

NOR
A GAY GLITTER
PALACE
IN
DRAG
CLOSET QUEENS
ANY-PHILE
PEOPLE WITH
PREFERENCES
WITHOUT LABELS

NOT
A RAH-RAH
COLLEGE BAR
WITH STONEY
BOYS ALL WITH
JEAN KNEES
RIPPED
JUST RIGHT
AND 'BOPPERS
VAMPISH BEYOND
THEIR
YEARS

NOR
AN EAST END
HILLBILLY
ELECTRIC
BLUEGRASS
TAVERN WHERE
THE TRUCKER DANCES
WITH HIS OLD LADY
SHE SMILING BENEATH
THE BLACK
EYE HE GAVE HER
THE NIGHT BEFORE

NOT
AN UPTOWN SWINGING
SINGLES
ONE NIGHT STAND
MATING GROUND
FULL OF BEAUTIFUL
WINNERS
AND LOSERS
EXECUTIVES ON THE
RISE AND
ON THE
MAKE

THE BRUNSWICK TAVERN CAN BE ALL
OF THESE

AND
MUCH
MUCH
MORE

ALBERT OVERSEES IT ALL
A LANDMARK, LIKE THE DRINKING HALLS
THAT SERVE THE BEER AND MAKE THE CLAIM:
NO OTHER PUB IS QUITE THE SAME.

CARLO KEEPS HIS HAT ON WHILE
HE SINGS; IT SHADOWS THE CHERUBIC
SMILE HE FLASHES LIKE BOLD
BLACKFACE IN A JOLSON MEDLEY
HE MAKES EVERYBODY
HOMESICK FOR THEIR
MAMMY   OH YEAH!

DONNIE SINCLAIR
HAS A VOICE
BIG AS ALL
OKLAHOMA.....
AND HE CAN
OUT-PELVIS
ELVIS.

PICKLE ALLEY IS THE PLACE TO HEAR
ALL THE OLD FAVOURITES, HAVE A BEER
OR TWO TO TOAST YOUR HEALTH
AND THEN GET UP AND SING
A FEW YOURSELF.

AND DOWN IN FRONT

SINGING RIGHT ALONG

BUT SILENTLY, LIP SYNC-ING

EVERY SONG

IS A LITTLE

RED-NOSED

ELFIN MAN

ALL GRINS AND

WAVING HANDS

INVITING

EVERYONE TO

HELP HIM TO DO HIS

OLD BOJANGLES

SLOW SOFT SHOE

CONVERSATION IS POSSIBLE
KEEP IT SIMPLE AND SHOUT
POINT-BLANK IN THE EAR
OR TRY LIP READING OUT.

RUM ᴀᴜ 80   BAR RUG. 80

TH
G

IVY THE HONKY-TONK QUEEN

SHE IS A PIXIE GAMIN WHO HASN'T
HEARD OF MIDDLE AGE
SHE SHOWS THE KEYS WHO'S BOSS AND
KEEPS THE STAGE ALIVE
WITH RITH'M TAPPING HEEL AND TOE
BOUNCING FIRST LADY OF THE BRUNSWICK SHOW.

CHICAGO:
WHO KNOWS WHAT
HE IS ABOUT,
NOT EVEN
ALBERT
SAYS IF HE DOES MORE
THAN JUST
HANG OUT.
ALWAYS ON THE FRINGES
STANDING BY OR
MOVING THROUGH
THE CROWD LIKE
SOMEONE
WHO WILL STOP
YOU DOIN' WHAT
AIN'T ALLOWED.

DRAFT BEER 30
BOTTLES   60

MISS EVE

SHE LIKES TO SING A COUNTRY KIND OF SONG
AND EVERYBODY CLAPS AND SINGS ALONG
BRIGHT RED HAIR, AND YELLOW RIBBONS IN THAT TREE
SHE SINGS IT FROM THE HEART SO NO ONE
CARES IF SHE'S A BIT OFF-KEY.

IN PICKLE ALLEY YOU CAN RELAX,
EVERYONE ALWAYS LOOKS AND ACTS
JUST AS THEY ARE, NO PRETENSE HERE
NOTHING FANCY BUT THE CHANDELIERS.

"MR. ENTERTAINMENT" PLAYS THE STICKS
CLACK-EY RITH'MS WHEN HE FLICKS
HIS WRISTS AND SHAKES HIS HANDS
A RHINESTONE STUDDED ONE-MAN-BAND

CONTEST NIGHTS
EVERYONE TURNS OUT
TO TRY THEIR SKILL
AT SOME OUTRAGEOUS
TASK, AND MAYBE WIN
A PRIZE, AND BASK
IN THE GLORY OF
THE BIGGEST
MOST, OR BEST
WHATEVER IS THE LATEST
BRUNSWICK TEST.

THE BALLAD OF THE GLASSEATING FRENCHMEN

ANY PUB IS ONLY AS GOOD
AS ITS BARMAIDS, IT'S GENERALLY UNDERSTOOD.
THIS TRUTH HAS NEVER BEEN TESTED AS WELL
AS THE NIGHT THOSE FRENCHMEN CAME IN AND RAISED HELL...
MOST MEN IN THEIR SHAPE WOULD
HAVE LONG SINCE PASSED OUT
WHEN THEY STARTED WAVING
THEIR BOTTLES ABOUT.
THEIR GLASSES WERE EMPTY
BUT RATHER THAN WASTE
THEM, THEY SALTED THE EDGES
AND GAVE THEM A TASTE.

THEY SAT MUNCHING GLASS
FOR FIVE MINUTES OR MORE
AND SPIT OUT THE GROUND
GLASS ALL OVER THE FLOOR....
THE BARMAID WALKED STOICALLY
OVER THE GRATE
AND HANDED THE FRENCHMAN
A TOWEL FOR HIS PLATE,
SHE KICKED A SMASHED BEER BOTTLE
OUT OF THE AISLE
AND WENT BACK TO HER ROUNDS
WITHOUT CRACKING A SMILE.

UPSTAIRS ALBERT
HAS
HIS HALL
DARKER
LIGHTS AND
TABLES
COUPLES ALL
ARRANGED
MORE INTIMATELY
DIGGING THE FIRST
CLASS JAZZ AND
DIXIELAND
PUT DOWN
BY "THE CLIMAX BAND".

THE MAN WITH
THE TROMBONE
PLAYS SHINY
GOLDEN
WAH-WAH
TONES;
LONG-ARMED
AND LANKY
SLIDING OUT THE NOTES
OR SLOUCHING FORWARD
OVER A
SHORT
SMOKE.

BANJO
SOLO STRUMMY
STRINGY ROAR
RAGTIME RAMBLING
COMING TO THE FORE,
PLANKY RITH'M
MOVES
YOUR SHOES,
PLINKY
BANJO BLUES.

WHEN THE BAND TAKES A BREAK
THE CROWD MAKES A DIN
THAT FILLS UP THE SPACE
WHERE THE MUSIC HAS BEEN;
THE JUKEBOX TAKES OVER
WITH HARDLY A LAPSE
GRINDING OUT RAUCOUS MUSIC
TO FILL ANY GAPS.

A LIQUID CLARINET

AND MELLOW

HORN; DUET

ROLLING UP AND

DOWN

THE SCALE;

SNAPPY BLUE

NOTES

AND A SILKY

WAIL.

ALL KINDS OF
PEOPLE
COME, PERHAPS
A BIT
MORE WELL-HEELED
THAN PICKLE
ALLEY REGULARS,
BUT WHEN THE
BAND HAS
DONE A SET
THEIR APPLAUSE
IS JUST AS ROWDY
AND EMPHATIC;
ANYTHING
ELSE WOULD BE
'ANTI-CLIMATIC'.

THERE IS A VERY POIGNANT
SAD OLD SONG
"THE CLIMAX BAND" PLAYS
JAZZY, LOUD AND STRONG.
AS IF APOLOGIZING
FOR ITS UP-BEAT FATE
THEY ALWAYS PAUSE
AND DEDICATE IT
TO THE SCHOOLTEACHER AND 'MAGGIE'
WHEN THE TWO OF THEM WERE YOUNG;
THEIR HOUSE IS AN HISTORIC SITE
OUTSIDE OF HAMILTON.

BIG NOISE

A SPECIAL BY TWO
MEMBERS
OF THE GROUP
ABOUT A TOWN
NOT FAR
PAST
"THE LOOP".
DON'T TAKE A MAP
AND TRY
TO FIND THE PLACE,
JUST SIT
BACK AND DIG
THE TISH
AND THUNK OF
DRUMS AND BASS.

THE BRUNSWICK TAVERN CAN BE ALL
OF THESE

AND
MUCH
MUCH
MORE